The Bermuda Triangle

by Jacqueline Laks Gorman

Gareth Stevens Publishing
A WORLD ALMANAC EDUCATION GROUP COMPANY

Please visit our web site at: www.garethstevens.com
For a free color catalog describing Gareth Stevens Publishing's
list of high-quality books and multimedia programs,
call 1-800-542-2595 (USA) or 1-800-387-3178 (Canada).
Gareth Stevens Publishing's fax: (414) 332-3567.

Library of Congress Cataloging-in-Publication Data

Gorman, Jacqueline Laks, 1955-
      The Bermuda Triangle / by Jacqueline Laks Gorman.
          p. cm. — (X science: an imagination library series)
      Includes bibliographical references and index.
      Summary: Provides an introduction to the accounts of mysterious happenings in an area
of the Atlantic Ocean known as the Bermuda Triangle.
      ISBN 0-8368-3196-9 (lib. bdg.)
      1. Bermuda Triangle—Juvenile literature. [1. Bermuda Triangle.] I. Title. II. Series.
G558.G67   2002
001.94—dc21   2002022536

First published in 2002 by
Gareth Stevens Publishing
A World Almanac Education Group Company
330 West Olive Street, Suite 100
Milwaukee, WI 53212 USA

Text: Jacqueline Laks Gorman
Cover design and page layout: Tammy West
Series editor: Betsy Rasmussen
Picture Researcher: Diane Laska-Swanke

Photo credits: Cover © Dezsö Sternoczky/SUFOI/Fortean Picture Library; pp. 5, 13, 15,
19 © Bettmann/CORBIS; p. 7 Tammy Gruenewald/© Gareth Stevens, Inc., 2002; p. 9
© Bruce A. Dale/NGS Image Collection; p. 11 © Mary Evans Picture Library; p. 17
© Museum of Flight/CORBIS; p. 21 NOAA Photo Library

Printed in the United States of America

3 4 5 6 7 8 9 10 09 08 07 06

Front cover: Did giant waves sink
some of the ships that have been
lost in the Bermuda Triangle?

TABLE OF CONTENTS

Words that appear in the glossary are printed in **boldface**
type the first time they occur in the text.

THE DISAPPEARANCE OF FLIGHT 19

One day in December 1945, five U.S. Navy planes that made up Flight 19 took off from Florida. The planes were on a training mission. They were supposed to be in the air for two hours, but, somehow, the planes and the fourteen people on board got lost.

Terrible radio messages came in from the flight leader. He said his **compasses** were not working, and he did not know where he was. The navy lost radio contact with the planes before anyone could tell the flight leader which way to go. The weather got worse. After five hours, Flight 19 disappeared. One search plane that was sent out to find the missing flight also disappeared.

The five navy planes that made up Flight 19 were called Avenger **torpedo** bombers. They probably ran out of fuel and crashed at sea. The search plane that disappeared may have exploded after takeoff.

LOST IN THE TRIANGLE

Flight 19 and the search plane were lost in a place called the **Bermuda** Triangle. People say thousands of ships and planes disappear for no reason in this area. They also say that, often, no **wreckage** or survivors are left behind.

The Bermuda Triangle is in the Atlantic Ocean. The three points of the Triangle are Florida, Bermuda, and Puerto Rico. Some people believe strange forces in the Triangle cause weird things to happen and make people confused. The compasses for the leader of Flight 19, for example, did not work when he was in the Triangle. The flight leader was reported as saying, "Everything looks wrong. Even the ocean looks strange."

The Bermuda Triangle's points are the islands of Bermuda in the north; San Juan, Puerto Rico, in the south; and the coast of Miami, Florida, in the west.

BERMUDA
ISLANDS
FLORIDA
BERMUDA
TRIANGLE
ATLANTIC OCEAN
CUBA
PUERTO
RICO
SOUTH AMERICA

HOW THE MYSTERY BEGAN

Many ships and planes pass through the Bermuda Triangle every year. Accidents happen because this area is so busy, and sometimes ships and planes have been lost in these accidents. No one thought the loss of ships and planes was strange until two men began to write about it. One man called the area the "Triangle of Death."

People started to look at the history of the area. They noticed that a mysterious place called the Sargasso Sea was inside the Triangle. Ships can just drift in this sea, because often there is no wind. Some people made long lists of every ship and plane that ever had problems in the Bermuda Triangle. The mystery and the myth about the Bermuda Triangle had begun.

The many islands that make up the Bahamas lie within the Bermuda Triangle. The islands' coastlines have many reefs and are popular among boaters and scuba divers.

FAMOUS LOST SHIPS

Christopher Columbus was caught in the Sargasso Sea in 1492, during his trip to the Americas. He saw odd lights over the water, and his ship's compasses did not work.

Columbus's ships got out of the Triangle, but others were not as lucky. The *Mary Celeste* was found drifting in the Triangle in 1872. Its captain, his family, and the eight-man crew were gone. In 1881, the British ship *Ellen Austin* found a ghost **schooner** — a ship drifting at sea. The captain of the *Ellen Austin* sent some of his crew to the schooner. The two ships drifted apart in a storm. According to some stories, the ships met again a few days later, and the men on the schooner had disappeared.

The *Santa Maria* was one of Christopher Columbus's three sailing ships. When the ships were in the Sargasso Sea, the crew got scared and wanted to sail home.

THE LOST TANKER

The *Marine Sulphur Queen* was a huge **tanker** that set sail in February 1963. It was traveling from Texas to Virginia, carrying a cargo of hot, liquid **sulfur**. The ship sent routine radio messages before it sailed into the Bermuda Triangle and disappeared, with all thirty-nine people aboard.

A few weeks later, some **debris** from the tanker was found. No one ever found out what happened. Did the sulfur on board explode? No **evidence** of an explosion was found. Perhaps the tanker ran into a storm, but if the tanker was in trouble, why didn't the crew send a distress call?

Members of the Coast Guard examine two life preservers and a foghorn from the *Marine Sulphur Queen* that were found off the coast of Florida.

MYSTERIOUS FORCES?

Some people blame **supernatural** forces for the strange things that have happened in the Bermuda Triangle. Some say aliens in UFOs are stealing ships and kidnapping the crews. Others blame **black holes**. Could it be that time warps are sending ships to another time or place, or that the lost city of **Atlantis** is sunk beneath the Triangle, sending out energy rays?

No one has yet found answers to all of the Triangle's mysteries. They do not know why compasses sometimes do not work, or why people sometimes lose radar and radio contact. According to some stories, gravity seems different inside the Triangle.

A C-119 Flying Boxcar disappeared in June 1965 in the Bermuda Triangle. Some said it was captured by a UFO.

ATTACKING THE MYSTERY

Many people think the Bermuda Triangle is just a myth. They say that many of the ships were not actually in the Triangle when they became lost.

According to many of the stories about the Triangle, wreckage and survivors were never found. Actually, many survivors *were* rescued. Some survivors said sudden storms caused them to abandon ship.

Also, many wrecks were found much later than their disappearances. Wreckage can be hard to find. The ocean is very deep and waves can be very high. Trenches, or great valleys, on the ocean floor can hide debris.

The nuclear submarine *Scorpion* was lost in May 1968. It is included in many lists of ships lost in the Bermuda Triangle, but the *Scorpion* was actually found many miles away.

WHAT IS THE TRUTH?

Scientists and other people offer many reasons to explain the cause of mysterious events that happen in the Bermuda Triangle. Strong storms can pop up suddenly and disappear just as quickly. There may be underwater earthquakes in the area. The Gulf Stream, an ocean current that flows through the Triangle, is very strong and can throw boats off course.

People may also be to blame. People can make mistakes while flying planes or piloting boats, especially when they do not have much experience.

Do these causes explain all of the lost ships and planes, or could something strange really be going on in the Bermuda Triangle?

This print from the 1850s shows a clipper ship caught in stormy seas off the coast of Bermuda. This area is often hit by unexpected thunderstorms, water spouts, and strong hurricanes.

CLIPPER SHIP "COMET" OF NEW YORK.

MORE TO READ AND VIEW

Books (Nonfiction) *The Bermuda Triangle.* Brian Innes (Raintree/Steck-Vaughn)
The Bermuda Triangle. Nathan Aaseng (Lucent Books)
DK Eyewitness Readers: Bermuda Triangle. Level Three: Reading Alone.
    Andrew Donkin (DK Publishing)
Mary Celeste: An Unsolved Mystery from History. Jane Yolen
    (Simon & Schuster)
The Mystery of the Bermuda Triangle. Can Science Solve (series).
    Chris Oxlade (Heineman Library)

Books (Fiction) *The Lost City of Balee.* Don Stafford (Pajo Publishing)
The Mystery of the Bermuda Triangle. Hey Arnold Chapter Book
    (series). Craig Bartlett and Maggie Groening (Simon Spotlight)

Videos (Nonfiction) *Beneath the Bermuda Triangle.* (New Horizons Home Video)
Bermuda Triangle — Incredible Mysteries. (Questar)
Bermuda Triangle — Secrets Revealed. (Questar)
Exploring Under the Sail: The Making of Treasure Island & the
    Bermuda Triangle. (Bennett Marine Video)
NOVA: The Bermuda Triangle. (Karen Voight)
UFO Diaries: Bermuda Triangle/Area 51. (Republic Studios)

Videos (Fiction) *Lost in the Bermuda Triangle.* (Paramount Studios)
The Triangle. (TBS Superstation)

WEB SITES

Web sites change frequently, but we believe the following web sites are going to last. You can also use good search engines, such as **Yahooligans!** [www.yahooligans.com] or **Google** [www.google.com] to find more information about the Bermuda Triangle. Some keywords that will help you are: *Bermuda Triangle*, *Triangle of Death*, *Mary Celeste*, and *Sargasso Sea*.

www.ajkids.com

Ask Jeeves Kids, the junior Ask Jeeves site, is a great place to do research. Try asking:

What is the Bermuda Triangle?

Where is the Sargasso Sea?

You can also just type in words and phrases with "?" at the end, such as:

Bermuda Triangle?

Atlantis?

www.yahooligans.com

Yahooligans! is the junior version of the Yahoo site. It is very easy to do searches here. Simply type in the words *Bermuda Triangle* to get a list of sites that are appropriate for kids.

www.bstar.net/bermudatriangle

This *Bermuda Triangle* site lays out the evidence, so you can decide for yourself if you believe in the mystery of the Bermuda Triangle.

www.unmuseum.mus.pa.us/triangle.htm

From the Museum of Unnatural Mystery comes the *Un-mystery of the Bermuda Triangle*, which gives information about the Bermuda Triangle.

www.bermuda-triangle.org

The *Bermuda Triangle* site is a complete site maintained by a journalist and active researcher who believes that unusual events occur in the Bermuda Triangle. This site has lots of material on different theories and investigations, as well as information about missing ships and planes.

octopus.gma.org/Tidings/myths/bermuda.html

This *Bermuda Triangle* site explains the legend of the Bermuda Triangle and also has a maze for you to escape from.

www.history.navy.mil/faqs/faq8-1.htm

The *Naval Historical Center* gives information about the Triangle area where ships and planes mysteriously disappear.

GLOSSARY

You can find these words on the pages listed. Reading a word in a sentence helps you understand the meaning of the word even better.

Atlantis (at-LAN-tihs) — a legendary island that is supposed to have sunk beneath the sea. 16

Bermuda (burr-MYOO-dah) — a group of islands in the western Atlantic Ocean. 6, 8, 12, 14, 16, 18, 20

black holes (BLAK HOHLS) — in space, the high-gravity areas around stars that have collapsed. 16

cargo (KAR-goh) — goods carried by a ship, plane, train, or truck. 12, 14

compasses (KUHM-puhs-es) — instruments used to find directions. 4, 6, 10, 16

debris (duh-BREE) — pieces left when something has been destroyed. 14, 18

evidence (EV-uh-dehns) — information or proof. 14

schooner (SKOO-nerr) — a sailing ship. 10

sulfur (SULL-fur) — a yellow substance used when making paper, rubber, some medicines, and other products. 14

supernatural (SOO-purr-NACH-ur-al) — involving something that cannot be explained by the laws of nature. 16

tanker (TANK-urr) — a ship, plane, or truck that has tanks to carry liquids. 14

torpedo (tohr-PEE-doh) — a missile that travels underwater to hit its target. 4, 12

wreckage (REK-ij) — the broken parts left after something has been badly damaged. 6, 18

INDEX